This book ~~belongs to:~~
is shared with

_____

_____

_____

a little light

to all who heal

© 2016 Conscious Stories LLC

Illustrations by Rosie Balyuzi

Published by
Conscious Stories LLC
1831 12th Ave South, Suite 118
Nashville, TN 37203

www.consciousstories.com

First Edition
Library of Congress
Control Number: 2017901962
ISBN 978-1-943750-09-2

The last 20 minutes of every day are precious.

Dear parents, teachers, and readers,

This story has been gift-wrapped with two simple mindfulness practices to help you connect more deeply with your children in the last 20 minutes of each day.

● Quietly set your intention for calm, open connection.

● Then start your story time with the **Snuggle Breathing Meditation**. Read each line aloud and take slow, deep breaths together in order to relax and be present.

● At the end of the story, you will find **The Light Switch**. This will help you and your child to reconnect to the bright light that shines inside. If you feel playful and radiant...then you have done it perfectly!

Enjoy snuggling into togetherness!

Andrew

Snuggle Breathing

Our story begins with us breathing together.
Say each line aloud and then
take a slow deep breath in and out.

I breathe for me

I breathe for you

I breathe for us

I breathe for all that surrounds us

Once upon a time,

there was a little light

who intended

to shine

a rainbow so bright.

It started to **GROW**

and learn all the things
he needed to know.

His little body seemed

perfectly equipped

with eyes
and ears
and hands

and legs
joined at
the hips.

9

But the bright
light inside

that intended
to shine

10

got clouded

as he grew

and was
harder to find.

Hmm...

He learned all the things
he needed to know ...

some of them were wrong

and blocked
up his flow.

The rainbow
lost its colors.

The path of light
went skew.

His perfect little body
coughed and
spluttered too.

So....

They took him
to the doctor

to fix his broken bits.

It helped
out a little,

but soon
returned in fits.

They took
him to the
therapist

to fix his broken mind.

He poked around a little.

There was
nothing
broken to find.

They took him
to the church

to fix his
broken soul.

They often looked at parts

and forgot
about the
WHOLE.

They took him
to a healer

to see what
she could find.

Thankfully,

the doctor, church,
and therapist
didn't mind.

Working as a team

seemed to do the trick.

The little light
grew brighter.

He didn't feel so sick.

These healers
worked with love

and balanced

wholeness too,

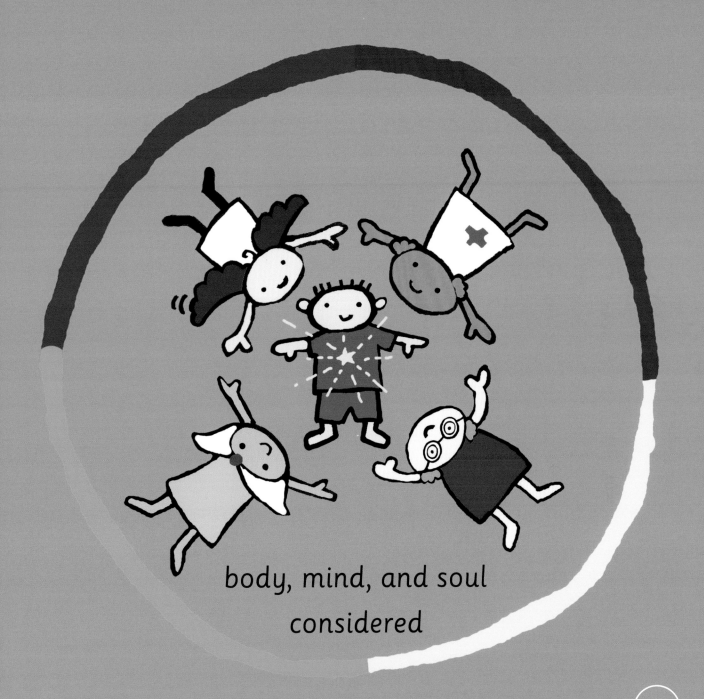

body, mind, and soul
considered

to help the
light shine through.

Yay!

You can shine!

Your personal light switch is deep in the middle of your belly. Follow these 4 steps before sleep, so that your light can recharge while you are resting.

You can do this any time you want to recharge.

Turn on your inner light
The Light Switch

1

Put your hands on the middle of your belly where your light lives.

2

Breathe in, saying, "I intend to shine brightly."

3

Let go of any
uncomfortable feelings
as you breathe out.

4

Stretch your
body.

5

Breath in while silently
saying your own name.

Sleep tight!

35

the collection

The Conscious Bedtime Story Club

snuggling into togetherness

the laughing witch

how diablo became Spirit

Anna Breytenbach & Andrew Newman

the tree of goodness

Andrew Newman

Rolling Thunder finds his herd

Andrew Newman

the elephant who tried to tiptoe

the boy who searched for silence

the dad who didn't know

Andrew Newman

we are circle people

Andrew Newman

the hug who got stuck

the sunburnt polar bear

the fish who searched for water

Andrew Newman

a little light

the bee who could not choose her flower

Andrew Newman

the girl with waterfall eyes

the forgetful elephant

Andrew Newman

the prayer who searched for God

Andrew Newman

Conscious Bedtime Stories

A collection of stories with wise and lovable characters who teach spiritual values to your children

Helping you connect more deeply in the last 20 minutes of the day

Stories with purpose

Lovable characters who overcome life's challenges to find peace, love and connection.

Reflective activity pages

Cherish open sharing time with your children at the end of each day.

Simple mindfulness practices

Enjoy easy breathing practices that soften the atmosphere and create deep connection when reading together.

Supportive parenting community

Join a community of conscious parents who seek connection with their children.

Free downloadable coloring pages
Visit www.consciousstories.com

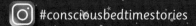 #consciousbedtimestories   @Conscious Bedtime Story Club

37

Andrew Newman - author

Andrew Newman is the award-winning author and founder of www.ConsciousStories.com, a growing series of bedtime stories purpose-built to support parent-child connection in the last 20 minutes of the day. His professional background includes deep training in therapeutic healing work and mindfulness. He brings a calm yet playful energy to speaking events and workshops, inviting and encouraging the creativity of his audiences, children K-5, parents, and teachers alike.

Andrew has been an opening speaker for Deepak Chopra, a TEDx presenter in Findhorn, Scotland and author-in-residence at the Bixby School in Boulder, Colorado. He is a graduate of The Barbara Brennan School of Healing, a Non-Dual Kabbalistic healer and has been actively involved in men's work through the Mankind Project since 2006. He counsels parents, helping them to return to their center, so they can be more deeply present with their kids.

TEDx **"Why the last 20 minutes of the day matter"**

Rosie Balyuzi - illustrator

Rosie Balyuzi has been an avid artist since the word go. She worked in production in the London animation industry in the nineties, specializing in children's TV shows such as "Noah's Island" and "The Adventures of Captain Pugwash." This sparked the flame to draw again as an adult, and she set up her own freelance design business called doodlehut. Through this venture, she has self-published and widely sold her own series of books, and also created badges t-shirts, and postcards. She now works as a freelance graphic designer and as a Swedish masseuse. Working with Andrew was her first collaboration as a children's book illustrator.

www.doodlehut.com

38

Star Counter

Every time you breathe together and read aloud, you make a star shine in the night sky.

Color in a star to count how many times you have read this book.